D1274332

david rosenberg
paris & london

books by David Rosenberg:

Excellent Articles of Japan
Disappearing Horses
A Head of Steam
Paris & London
A Star in my Hair
Leavin' America

talonbooks
1911 acadia road
vancouver 8
british columbia
canada

AFTERNOON

In the branches the light
so that the limbs
go out
on the moss
patient
my cares
o nature – ah! less alone
strange
the earth
should clothe me
with my shadow
nothing at all deceives me
it takes just everything
we have
to conceive this

THE ARGUMENT

Outside the french window
french door window
a whole 'nother culture
little girls going to school
little white dogs
clouds out for a stroll
you don't need me
you don't need abstract art
here, eat this photo
behind the glass
and the warmer air
and the softer light

POCKMARKS

All eyes
take me out walking
my frivolous
idol
primitive head
flesh like evening
like indolence
we know the caress
rose hips are enamoured of,
languid sunset poses
dark bites and kisses are lavished on
– on my heart
gentle as the moon
under the satin slippers
of my spirit
all light and color
an explosion
an afternoon gone

STANDING ON THE CORNER

You see a well-worn rag
unlucky cloud
perfect pearl
you let yourself get stoned
teardrops are falling on your head
Crusoeing thru romances
a pale streetlamp
passes a young girl
on a boulevard island
that lady vanishes
on lips of cement
in a blazing raft of identity

FLYING AWAY FROM HOME

All this language passin thru the air
that's where I am
jumping
the tape level meter
someone is screaming
'come together!'
Gladys Knight?
Paris filled with gentle ghosts
especially when it's sunny
the air a golden telephone
filled with faint praises
you just can't bother picking up

OLD PHOTO

(Black Bathroom 1962 Jim Dine postcard)

i.e. getting from china to here
(hair)
a good country mile
or two oo
getting a load off
a fast boat
& leaving it hanging in space
you can see
ain't back there

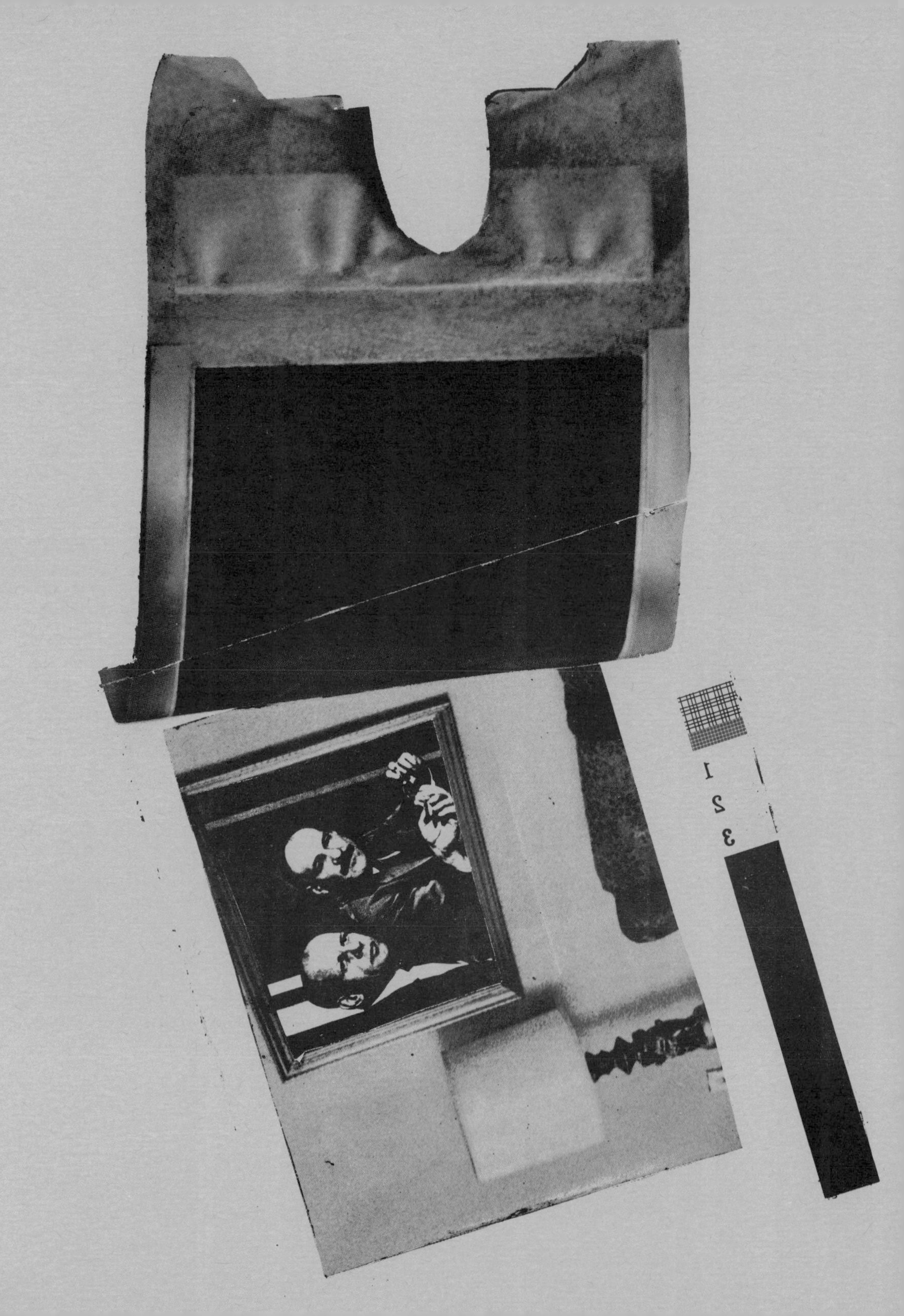

AMERICAN POETRY

taking a turn thru history
awhile
& found the celebrities of modern painting
hanging around backstage
in cheap prints
like badly spelt
little books for children
who grow old in another country
yes I dreamed of crusades
moving religious wars
racing continents
A black, *E* white
I red, *O* blue, *U* green
we find ourselves
in another moving language
translated at night in a hurry
like Hollywood subtitles
somewhere over the rainbow

WORK SONG

I went off with my hands
beneath the sky, Muse!
loves I dreamed of
a big hole in them
I sewed badly
with stars stitched in the sky
and I listened to them
dew on my forehead
cheap wine
into shadows I must pluck
like black shoelaces
one foot close to my heart

NIGHT SCHOOL

Let's not turn
back to
"I am lost"
What a great life!
ah! forgiveness!
just how many more
"I was born"
the one
at the bottom
under the deuce
that I am
permitted for life
to, this sea clam
bridegroom
cramped virgin
in a phantom opera
she can't kill me
and *I* can't
please
all of you
widows
a) skeleton!
b) child!
c) human being!
true math is elsewhere
yo' lost soul
lost in a simple man

don't like some women
that is sure
with hearts in each breast
with the food
of happiness
devoured from the start
turning a cruel thing into
a charm: her body
caucasian tattoo in space
over that body goes me
selflessly
a fly in the room
jewel against the moon
I treasure
light pupils

SUNNY BRIGHTLINGSEA

(from *Sky Lines*)

All those big city nights
laying about together
about two paces down memory lane
well cut my throat!
shaving in an air of crime
tender idiom
to those less fortunate
partings which rend
we used to get drunk??
... night which surrounded us
like cattlefences
with the pity of a mother
with the pretty airs of a little girl
on way to catechism
or business art
you could see the whole future
so much furniture
yes everything really touched
packed tight against the window
the sperm crashed on thru
out of a fading herd of stars
and lit up the sky
and all the folks on that lane
was born again

dec. 17

dear .....

reading thru back issues of Kulcher today, running thru time, and surprised how little resistance there is in it, especially going thru the numbers between O'Hara's art chronicle & where Ted & Ron come in at no. 16 or 17. So it was mostly reading Ted & Ron's letters & reviews & stories & art chronicle. That helped me up over the horrible suction in the midsection that's there when you're prying apart from a loved one. But there's still that delicate balance between the vertical forces and horizontal one. I guess the sitting in a chair is it, especially with your feet on the desk like when you're reading what you wrote, that way part of you is vertical and part horizontal and all of it balancing on a pinhead in space which is where you wrote that poem, your heart sucked into your mouth. It's safer there, I guess, then in a dress

flung at yr feet

you walk right over

so as to get upstairs

lie down in the attic

with the old letters

of love & faith

still in their envelopes

like stars in a constellation

crazy hot numbers

keep *away* from me

LULLABY

rest on (old soul)
I must help others
it is my duty

in the grip
in the darkness
of a lover's promise

space
as meaningless as
"I don't think so"

as a sleepwalker
no rights in world of reality
condition into

we all stumble
stones of unknown towns
customs will have changed

so will my taste
in children's books
(will *you* give it to me?)

(I don't know what)
hopes: but they can't be about me
(don't know how to pay)

you see that little dish down there?
woman?
saint?

AWAKE
up to pure prospect
upstairs with kittens

PLANT PSYCHOLOGY

(Essex University)

two steps and you're up
1. light up
2. wake up
tea or coffee
single return
healthy thoughts in a green bus
it's spring come back all over again
and you fall
light as a leaf
toward the education complex
downhill
and you have a mind to

ANCIENT NURSE

Lady
without too much
a white dress
clear as a diamond
breathed on by a sick patient
pearly sky
your brow
infinite space behind
a singular arab grace
cool thoughts
natural, far-off
and near white
like sand
with a moon reflected in each facet
suggests the diamond's forever
dazzling smile
plunging into the future
another night sky
that bare logic
pure shape
so vast a body
for my head so tiny
falling asleep on two shoulders
counting white hairs
falling stars
on the stairway
to the stars

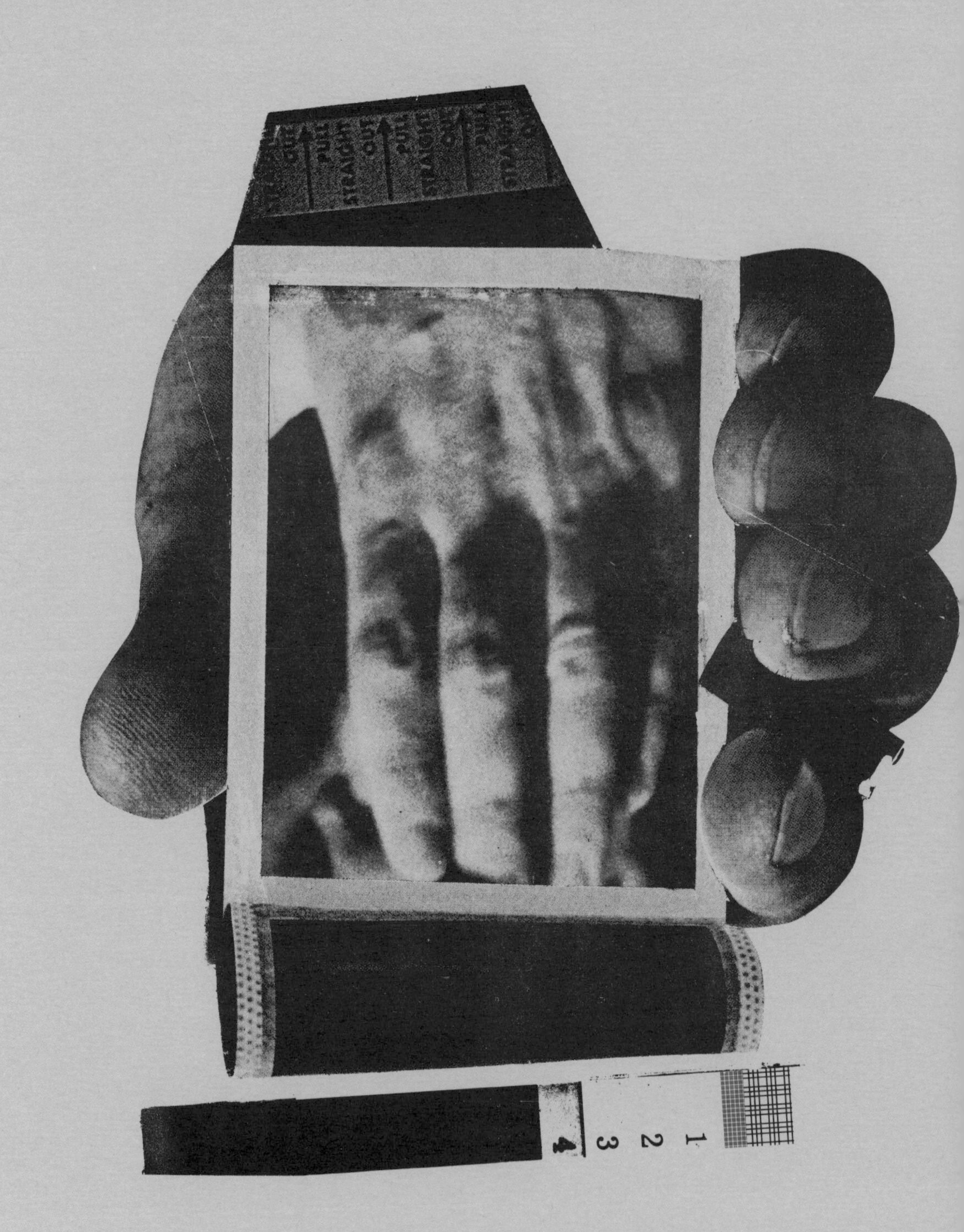
PULL STRAIGHT OUT
1
2
3
4

MISS SMITH

It's only love can break your heart
the world fall apart
100 feet beneath your feet
halfway thru the hole to china
up here it's rock 'n roll
one cut after the next
black 'n blue
and red like valentines
you leave your body to get
heart *and* soul
some unimaginable 1991 *Angel Hair*
cover by Jim Dine
rinky-tinky-tink
needle and thread
Fletcher Henderson's Hot Six

YANKEE DOODLE

Hang on to your life
life life
context is everything
last round
Allah is there
in the square garden
army sgt Jim Collins
spinnin you round on AFN
it's not who you are
but *where*
tuned to The Guess Who
fast in your seat
on land, sea, or air
you're way out in front
and you ain't going anywhere

DRUG CULTURE

Eiffel Tower
old ad for Paris
still draws the buses
"O.K. Paris"
words in any language
but that bus a dumb German
let's see what else I can bite into
it's lonely being her camera
when you're hungry
marijuana is false inspiration
true inspiration
is the in-drug with academics
you get it on top the Eiffel Tower
struck dumb by a an ad
for uh uh uh
say teach
you a motherfuckin asshole
am I right or wrong

ART HISTORY

holes in the walls
bullet-holes
your paintings hid
sure, I'll pay the price
& go thru this marked-up life
twice
you say goodbye
and I say hello
do you want francs or dollars
nuts
in my head
still attached to the bolts
so why can't we
because we go our own ways
like turn-of-the-century airplanes
thru those holes in the walls
into the textbook
cold air

FIRST LOVE

I said to her
"I understand you"
my grief is continual
as others would have it
everyone!
goodbye *kisses*
to a darkening heaven
getting the habit of it
good children stay at home
they are suited to one
not to a piercing
Singer sewing machine
that quiets down at night
your mouth on my heart
still open

SOFT WOMAN

any woman
who sees clearly
the interjection of flowers
excuses me from the effort of uttering a word
aloud
contrary
to this fortuitous proximity
the dimple
the sunbeam
on the face of the clock.
an evening falling over
in all ways at once
laughter of things
matter of facts
I have no idea
in the face
of *existence*:
meeting-place
where flowers grind to a halt!
mind: her words
shock absorbers
on a driving spirit
lit up at night
in a field of gravel

WHITE NIPPLE

She was very much half-dressed
against the clear pane
in my big
delicate feet
I watched a little wild
a breast was spinning
somewhere in the universe
& she laughed softly
a string of clear trills
on her petticoat
white moon
lake with birds over it
I kissed her twinkling eyes
as I started to count them
'Please sir, wait, I
have something to say to you'
inspiring maternal breast!
against you
impatient toes
open out
to another earth

BRIGHTLINGSEA SOUNDS GOOD

Assuming an art world is really out there
thanks for your letters & poems
winter approaching

this hot-line realist
somebody in Brightlingsea
looking at *Asylum Poems*

negative takes
like the Japanese Duck Pop
(you pull the duck inside out thru its own asshole)

here's the tentative table of contents
then off to Ratners
Stevie Winwood at the next table

(big dairy restaurant)
"culture"-consciousness seems inspiring
(Rivers? Warhol? Johns?)

I sort of remember where that is
Life in New York ... easy to get inio
makes you wonder where you'll go with it

some birds are chirping
"A Hundred Locomotives in The Roundhouse"
now working in Bolinas

north of San Francisco
something like 8 a.m.
1:30 in New York

how far is the nearest Guston?
"At Home With The Berrigans"
Brightlingsea sounds good

as Joyce said a pier is a disappointed bridge
"Young Writers Say They Don't Read"
so what is going on OUT THERE

: an occasional "head"
"We All Come From The Stars"
a record player, for instance

in Clark Coolidge's "reductive" style
untyped up
Meanwhile, Larry and Lewis have been collaborating alot

driving around and smoking in Guston's image-field all along
the scholarship scene
104 Greenwich Ave

a gloved hand pointing in from an edge
a little writer's block
round & round & round

Tom Clark says the indeterminate plot ricochets
"Dear Tom"
Bobby Seale went on trial yesterday, for murder, in New Haven

LONDON PRODUCTIONS

I just go out of my top
in here in the pop
where the pipe is warm
"at least it's centrally-heated"
takes snowshoes going thru
white hopes of London
& you wake up & it's gone
you can't go on this way
lovin' you
by 'you' you mean 'me'
& like writing your own anthology
the strongest thoughts get thru
narry a pat on the head
a tap on the bone
it's only make believe
no. 20 this week
might go down & get me a ticket
to montreal toronto or vancouver
whichever comes first
on the dial
in the sky
a dog is baying
out the bay window
let him bay
no commercials at least
I hear you knockin'
coffee or tea
the one that costs the most
it's "russian" tea with lemon
& you have to take the lemon
at least you know where you stand in nyc
you just have to know
if they're streets or avenues

by 'you' I mean 'we'
in between
listening to the third ear band
third album
let's hope they don't go off the deep end
we still want some more
American Beauty
to dry off on
underneath us
the 'you' of us
slippin' 'n slidin'
it's the 'fifties
anyone can see you wrote it as if it was then
it was
it was
soon as I get me a new address
out of the old phonebook
in Youngstown
black plastic with white dots
here & there
outside the window there
outside the door
outside Ohio
in a movie
"Savage Innocence"
I get killed in the end
by a camera falling on me

CLEAN SKIES

To daydream
in unmoving sky
idle bath
bluish
cut by shiny aircraft
floating white pieces
that as if they lived
sleep
thru the sunset
artistic
psychoanalysed
in appropriate light
up time
exquisitely chosen
for this our atmosphere
where smaller hothouses
minds
hover over blinking windows
we look on thru
impatient to be outside
on the palanquin of a sunny day
keeping up
above those Joneses
thru into dusk
and out to eyes which I can recognize
they vanish
on contemplation
those sable stars
what we commonly call life
in outer space
where the sun also rises
in the same constellation
every night

eternity reigns
a thump on the door
of my stomach
calls its servant to breakfast
to the suffering of The Times
another installment
somewhere over a shoulder
Judy Garland predicted
tap dancing on the window
switched on across the room
among idiotic bits of furniture
crossed out or forgotten
on the sheet
another day takes off
with the kitchen clock
automatic pilot
sweeping away
every living moment

FLIGHT BUSINESS

You see this big map spread out
under soft white flashes
the Atlantic
Joe Frazier in depth
I starts smoking him
Sicherheitsaüsrustung
Finest Extra Quality
good practice to be acquainted with them
dry land – Iceland?
white miniskirts
white pillows
By Appointment
His Late Majesty
sorry, this seat is ...
under front of your seat ...
Made in Canada
in white plastic
thru yellow champagne
you think this is easy
you idiot salesman
dumb ad for living
propped against carton of Rothmans
this is where I get off
Virginia

CAPITAL

(from *Sky Lines*)

Sturdy nobility
in no hurry
bourgeois consciences
like a summer night
out
at an infinite burlesque house
there are some
with planet patrons
moving on a day to day basis
with the night shows
These old fans are put out
just when it gets real hot:
the industrial pollution
pomading the hair
on nouveau riche studs
roaring out of the wings
on wheels
under invented lights

SLEEPING IN YOUR BOUGHS

Spring is evidently here
my heart wide open
O May!
O Arthur!
I'll listen to Art's tom-toms
cutting across the lake
bloodstained water
tumbling yellow heads
extra de luxe dawns
Cupid air
in Corot landscapes
I love the trees
they're familiar
not your unblinking irises
your heavenly cologne O Mother!
lighting up the parts
the white men play,
spraying your white hair green

IMAGINATION

I have a little cat blue
I like to take soft steps in her
on the forbidden grass of Paris
Les pelouses sont interdites aux chiens

THE WHITE TUXEDO

Sometimes she's gonna cry
and you won't know why

and you won't ask
you won't even own a necktie

to hang yourself up with
you'll be totally normal

you won't want to die
like an ordinary housefly

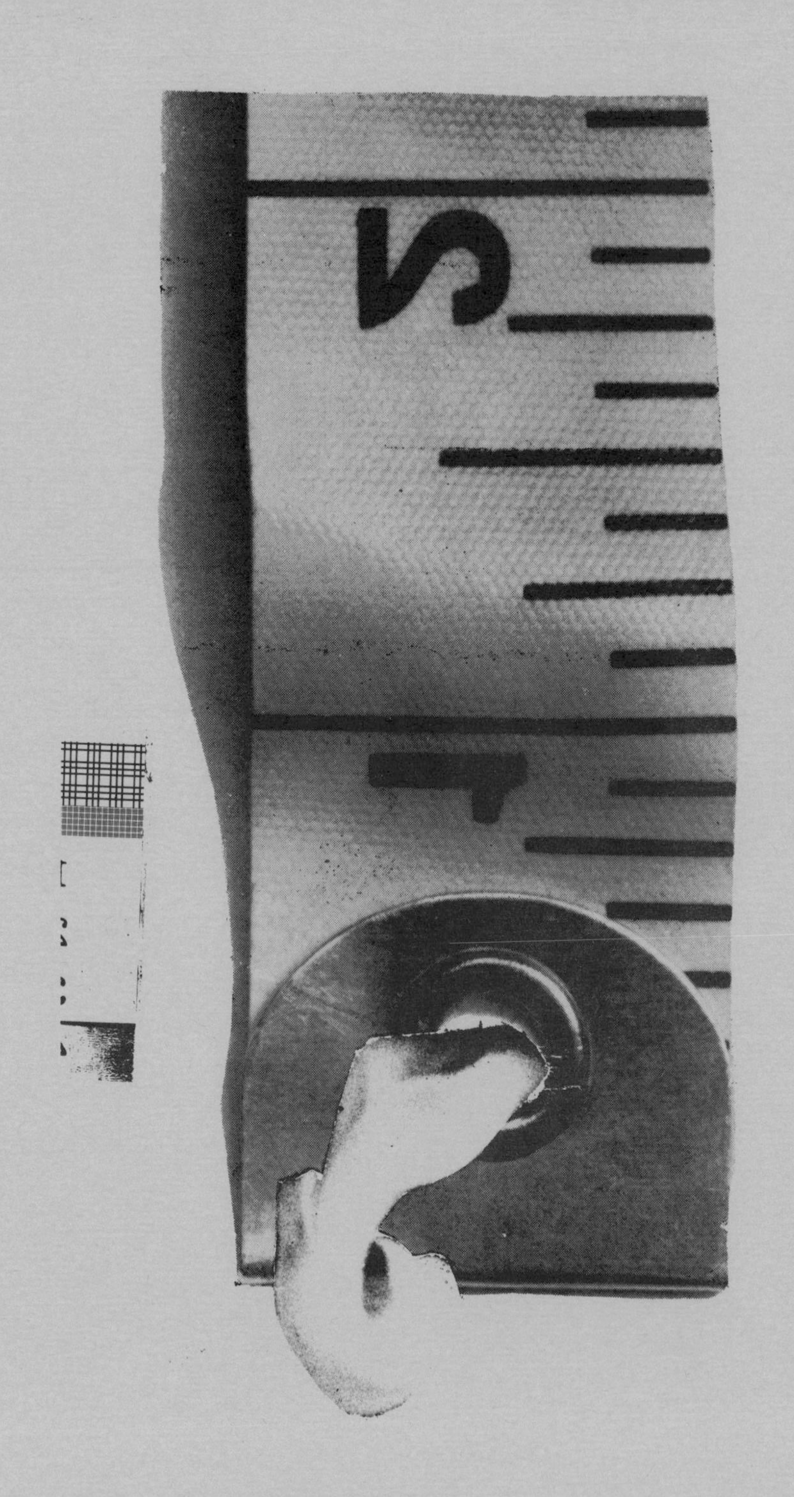

SMOKING THRU THE DARK

Sometimes it gets so hard to sigh
so far out high

anyway what does "hard" mean?
the nearest burnt out star?

when along comes your baby
the Gitanes with the filter

you set her aflame
you're her one man solar system

GO FUCK YOURSELF

you are a shit.
your body is shit.
all you want to do is sleep with your poems
with a body with an ego

WHITE CURTAINS

It's all a matter of getting past words to the language outside our head, either visually like art or orally like poetry. Because words are inadequate, in this programmed space, to get through the machines, you have to come out from behind them and make a dash for the border just as they stop at the first security check. This is what is commonly known as "Checkpoint Charlie".

HERMAN MELVILLE

October 13, 1970 to November 4, 1970

LA FIN DU MONDE

Arlette

je t'aime

quelq'un dira le grand Amour

ayant le ciel bleu pour ciel-de-lit

qu'elle pleure à présent sous les remparts

oh! bras trop courts!

le monde est vicieux

la lune de miel cueillera leur sourire

je suis le savant au fauteuil sombre

ce ne peut être que la fin du monde

je te connais et t'admire

en silence

7 AP

(memo: must write to John
(James)
could be doing it now Dear John
I am just escaping from your book

it was a very strong tank
but awkward in the modern warfare of silence
it's war I'm writing not (style)
so come out from behind that grassblade

I can't hurt you I'm only a man
talking to the walls
of your gaseous patience
If I say 'I love you'

that is like a Kaiser-Fraser
beeping for recognition
in the prison compound of history
Next door to the world

my *true* love is so calm
her heart is idling
because I rarely step on the gas
that nevertheless fills her patience

and drives me up the walls
If this is still World War I
this tear gas is for you Gaudier
Get back into John's poem this instant

I want to go home in style
open the door sit down and appreciate
April as she whittles the rifle butts
of the silent days in 1970

hum like an automatic writing
and let you check my oil
and Arthur Rimbaud my ethyl
beatrice to you Gerard Malanga I would write

to you but the truth in this poem is sleeping
Now John if you could just help me over this hill
12:01.   thanks.
And thank you for giving this poem your hand.

OUT OUEST

GREAT of roy to allow me this space
in vancouver tho
where I'll sleep tonite don't know

if I can
who 'wants' me
smokin CRAVEN "A"

something else no brand name
one day proved
impossible to live with her on daily basis

a night recovered
canada's mildest
need car in vancouver

all the next years models
of fifties fading sculpture
still visible like nowhere

in the world
charcoal pink black & white
on one de soto

endless 55 chevys
that change after 54
blew my mind

falling in love in detroit
poking under canvas covers
in GM garage on paper route

sat thru some legal marriages
great vaudville between
be nice to have a quiet home
and a kid and a couple cats
david's life – tree
up country canada
on gerry's new *Lease*
he read it out
we took it in
I was looking at carol's eggs
wanting her whole
all true models forever

AN AMERICAN PAINTING

If I'm right then you must be
Comrade Wrong
hi mister!
I'm a cute little thing
my stockings
roll down to Laredo
my twat is like Passaic Falls
a man contemplates all his life
hi willy!
(stepped right thru him)
& tripped over Berrigan knee
& fell into Anne's twat
Ted came in & I asked him
What poets you like best?
Ted struck a match
as if he was dusting furniture
in galaxy X
I like ANYTHING in poetry
that huge viewpoint blew my mind
a moment
then walked past Peace Eye
noting '67 plate on buick parked out front
it was blue
under a field of stars
then George turned to Martha
pulled out his cock
stuck it in empty inkwell
I saw it still there this morning
then a brushstroke of light
wiped out my mind

This book was designed in collaboration with David Rosenberg by
David Robinson. It was printed by Gordon Fidler in August, 1971.
The cover and endpapers were printed at The Coach House Press.

The illustrations are by David Bolduc.

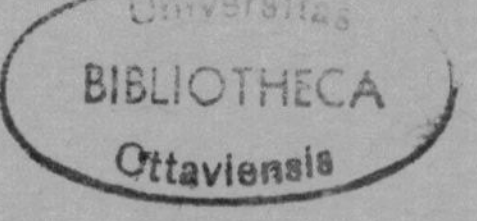